P9-DXG-952

SOLVING MYSTERIES WITH SCIENCE

BIGFOOT
AND THE
YETI

MARY COLSON

Raintree
Chicago, Illinois

Edited by Adam Miller, Vaarunika Dharmapala, and
Claire Throp
Designed by Ken Vail Graphic Design
Original illustrations © Capstone Global Library Ltd
2014
Illustrated by Chris King
Picture research by Mica Brancic
Production by Victoria Fitzgerald
Originated by Capstone Global Library Ltd
Printed and bound in China by CTPS

17 16 15 14 13
10 9 8 7 6 5 4 3 2 1

**Library of Congress Cataloging-in-Publication
Data**
Colson, Mary.
  Bigfoot and the Yeti / Mary Colson.
    p. cm.—(Solving mysteries with science)
  Includes bibliographical references and index.
  ISBN 978-1-4109-5499-2 (hb)—ISBN 978-1-4109-
5505-0 (pb) 1. Sasquatch—Juvenile literature. 2.
Yeti—Juvenile literature. I. Title.

QL892.2.S2C65 2013
001.944—dc23   2012042238

Acknowledgments
We would like to thank the following for permission to
reproduce photographs: Alamy pp. 23 (© Mary Evans
Picture Library), 28 (© Sherab); FLPA p. 24 (Frans
Lanting); Getty Images pp. 18 (Gallo Images/Danita
Delimont), 21 (Dorling Kindersley), 27 (Popperfoto),
36 (Workbook Stock/Gary Mccue), 37 (PhotoLink/C.
McIntyre), 32–33; Museum of Man, San Diego p.
29; Newscom p. 41 (Bigfoot Global LLC); Press
Association Images p. 39 (AP); Rex Features pp. 16
(Associated Newspapers/Jim Hutchison), 40 (Alastair
Pullen), 25 bottom (Sipa Press), 42; Shutterstock pp.
4–5 (© Charles Masters), 16–17 (© Valentyn Volkov),
18–19 (© Vicki France), 20 (© Gary Yim), 22–23 (©
Gucio_55), 25 top (© XYZ), 27 (© Daniel Loretto), 28
(© Rachel Blaser), 30–31 (© Jason Patrick Ross), 36
(© Dmitry Strizhakov), 40–41 (© BGSmith); Top Foto
pp. 30, 31, 34 left, 34 right 35.

Background design images supplied by Shutterstock
(© nrt), (© argus), (© Vitaly Korovin).

Cover photograph of a man in a yeti costume
reproduced with permission of Rex Features (Sipa
Press) and the footmark of a yeti reproduced with
permission of Alamy (© TP).

CONTENTS

BIGFOOT AND THE YETI: AN UNSOLVED MYSTERY

All over the world, people tell stories of strange ape-like creatures or wild men. In parts of North America, people tell of unexpected encounters with a giant, hairy human-ape called Bigfoot, while in the snowy mountains of the Himalayas, unexplained giant footprints and sightings in the snow lead locals to believe in, sometimes worship, and fear the yeti.

One thing that is certain is that the mysterious wild ape-man is an important cultural figure in folklore from Australia and China to Europe and North America. These creatures have been blamed for violent murders and animal thefts, in addition to appearing as "bogeymen" figures in cautionary tales. Some people believe that they even have supernatural powers.

Solving the mystery?

The first part of this book looks at some Bigfoot and yeti stories. The second part of the book uses science to ask questions about the evidence, to look at the theories, and to prove or disprove the existence of such creatures. Can science solve the mysteries of these huge ape-men of the mountains and forests?

▼ Could a yeti live here?

NAMING THE BEAST

Throughout the Himalayas, a mysterious creature has many different names. *Yeti* is the most common and is sometimes translated as "that thing" in the Sherpa language. In Tibetan, *Yeti* means "magical creature," while in North America, Bigfoot is also called "Sasquatch" and "Oh-man-ah." All the names refer to a wild, human-bear or ape from legends.

THE KIDNAPPING OF ALBERT OSTMAN

In a hot and humid Canadian police station in August 1957, 64-year-old Albert Ostman wearily sat down. He was going to finally tell his story, a story that he had kept secret for over 30 years...

DREAMING OF GOLD

In 1924, young Albert wanted adventure and wealth. Like many others, he hoped to strike gold and had already been prospecting (searching) in many places, but with no luck. He had recently read about an old gold mine near a place called Toba Inlet, in a remote part of Canada. He set off to find his fortune.

LONELY WILDERNESS

Toba Inlet is in British Columbia, Canada, a province about twice the size of California. Then, as now, it was one of the least populated places on Earth, and Albert found himself alone in this vast, lonely landscape. Each night, he slept fully dressed, with his gun and knife in his sleeping bag for protection.

...all he knew was that he had to escape...

RUDE AWAKENING

One night, as he lay sleeping under the stars by the remains of his dying campfire, Albert woke up with a jolt. Something had picked him up and was carrying him off in his sleeping bag! For three hours, Albert was carried, dragged, and bumped across the land by a stinky creature before being put down. As Albert slowly peered out of his bag, he saw a sight that he could not quite believe. There, staring down at him, stood a family of four Bigfoots, two of them around 8 feet (2.4 meters) tall.

CAMP BIGFOOT

Rubbing his eyes in disbelief, Albert stared at the Bigfoots. All covered in hair, they looked like giant apes. They seemed to be talking to each other, but Albert couldn't understand what they were saying.

LIFE WITH BIGFOOT

The days passed, and Albert survived by eating sweet grass roots. He watched the Bigfoot family as they looked for food and added leaves to the inside of their den. They let him walk around their little area, but they would not let him out of their sight.

Albert did not even know where he was; all he knew was that he had to escape. Warily, patiently, he watched and waited for his chance.

FAST ESCAPE!

On the sixth day, Albert fed the largest Bigfoot some tobacco. The Bigfoot did not like it and ran off. Albert sped toward the camp entrance, shooting at the other Bigfoots and scaring them away. He ran into the trees, down into the valley, and made his way to safety.

HIDDEN SECRET

Albert didn't tell anyone about his experience, fearing he would be thought crazy. Eventually, he could keep it secret no longer and told the police. On August 20, 1957, Albert was declared officially sane by police magistrate A. M. Naismith, to whom he had told his tale.

BEHEADED BY BIGFOOT?

In 1906, brothers Willie and Frank McLeod searched for gold near Nahanni River in northern Canada. Two years later, their headless bodies were discovered. Their mysterious deaths were blamed on a Bigfoot, and the place was renamed Headless Valley.

THE STORY OF THE SHEPHERDESS

In the same year that Albert Ostman was telling his tale, something very frightening was happening on the other side of the world...

One afternoon, in Zhuantan, a remote village in eastern China, a shepherdess tended her herd of cattle. Xu Fudi and her daughter did this every day, moving the animals to the best grazing areas.

BLOOD-CURDLING SCREAMS

Suddenly, the little girl screamed out in horror. Xu Fudi's blood ran cold as she turned and saw a giant ape-like creature carrying her daughter away. The tall, strong creature had long brown hair. Its eyebrows, ears, and tongue were like a man's, with a flat nose and a wide, large chest. Xu Fudi froze before she pulled herself together and chased the beast.

As she ran after her daughter, Xu Fudi's cries were heard by other women from the village. Xu Fudi grabbed a branch and began beating the creature until it dropped her daughter who, miraculously, was unhurt. The other women brought sticks and brooms with them and, together, they beat the creature until it was dead.

The women took its hands and feet back to the village to show other people. They were pickled to preserve them, to warn others of the dangerous beast.

CABIN ATTACK!

In July 1924, five miners were working near Mount St. Helens in Washington state. As they worked and moved around the area prospecting, they noticed some large footprints on the ground, which were about 19 inches (48 centimeters) long. The miners could not think of any animal that could have made them...

SCARY SOUNDS

At night, from outside the miners' windowless wooden cabin, a shrill whistle pierced through the darkness. Other strange panting and breathing noises were coming closer. Then, the unnerved men heard a thumping sound, as if an animal were hitting itself on its chest.

A SHOT THROUGH THE TREES

One day, two of the men went to get some water from a nearby stream. Spooked by the prints and the noises, they took their rifles with them for safety. Suddenly, about 300 feet (90 meters) away on the other side of a little canyon, they saw a 7-foot- (2.1-meter-) tall hairy creature. In panic, the men shot three times. The creature ran away and disappeared. Or so the men thought, as they hurried back to their cabin...

SHRIEKS AND SMELLS

Many sightings of both Bigfoot and the yeti report that the creature stinks! People also report hearing strange screams. On January 15, 2001, a camper in Wissahickon State Park, in Pennsylvania, was startled awake by ear-piercing shrieks. As he peered out of his tent, he saw a tall, almond-colored creature about 82 feet (25 meters) away. There was also a dreadful skunk-like stench coming from the creature.

STICKS AND STONES!

Around midnight, the five men were woken by a tremendous thud against the cabin wall and a terrifying howling. The whole building shook, as something outside pounded the walls and hurled stones. One of the men recalled, "The creatures were pushing against it and the whole door vibrated from the impact."

Leaping out of their beds, the frightened men quickly braced the door with a long pole from a bunk bed. Through chinks in the cabin's wooden walls, the men could see three Bigfoots. In the darkness inside, they fumbled for their guns. There was another mighty thud against the walls, and it felt like the cabin would be pushed over.

The next thing they knew, one of the Bigfoots had climbed onto the roof! The men started shooting upward, hoping to kill the creatures or at least scare them away.

CABIN DEFENSE

Suddenly, a large, hairy arm reached through a space in the cabin wall and grabbed an axe! One of the miners, Fred Beck, quickly turned the head of the axe upright, so that it caught on the logs. The Bigfoot let go, and Fred pulled the axe back in.

The attack continued for the rest of the night, with the five men huddled together inside the cabin.

PACK AND RUN!

Just before daylight, the attack ended. When they were sure it was safe, the miners came cautiously out of the cabin. They packed what supplies and equipment they could carry and left.

...a large, hairy arm reached through a space in the cabin wall and grabbed an axe...

THE MYSTERY OF THE CREATURE IN THE SNOW

In 1925, photographer N. A. Tombazi was on the Zemu Glacier in the Himalayas. He was climbing at around 15,000 feet (4,600 meters) when he noticed something moving on the mountain. He recalled, "The figure in outline was exactly like a human being, walking upright and stopping occasionally...It showed up dark against the snow, and as far as I could make out, wore no clothes." A little further on, he saw some giant footprints in the snow. Tombazi took photographs, but he saw nothing more of the creature.

▲ Don Whillans saw a strange beast in the Himalayas. Could it have been a yeti?

Forty-five years later...

In 1970, mountaineer Don Whillans was attempting to achieve a lifetime's ambition—to scale the mighty mountain of Annapurna in Nepal.

Mountain camp

Don was climbing with a local Sherpa guide. They were making good progress when they decided to stop for the night and set up camp on the mountain.

While Don was scouting for a suitable campsite, he heard some strange cries. His guide said they belonged to a yeti. Don nodded and thought nothing more of it as he hurried to get their tents set up before dark.

Shape in the shadows

Later that night, Don saw a dark shape moving near his tent. The next day, he observed a few giant footprints in the snow. That evening, through his binoculars, Don saw an ape-like creature moving across the snow. He watched it for 20 minutes, and it seemed to search for food before it disappeared from view. Throughout the rest of his trip, he did not see the creature again.

INVESTIGATING BIGFOOT AND THE YET!

For over 2,000 years, people have been reporting sightings and encounters with yetis and Bigfoots. In the 4th century BCE, Alexander the Great was warned about yetis in the mountains surrounding the Indus Valley. More recently, Bigfoot sightings are reported every couple of months, but there is no concrete proof—yet.

Can the mysteries of Bigfoot and the yeti be solved? Do the stories and reports of strange, wild ape-men in the mountains stand up to scientific investigation?

▶ In medieval Europe, people told stories about the woodwose, a hairy wild man.

WILDMEN OF THE WORLD

Stories of giant wild men abound in many cultures. The woodwose of medieval Europe, the Chinese Yeren, the Australian Yowie, and the Alma of Central Asia all share the same characteristics: hairy, giant, mysterious, wild ape-like creatures. But are they mythical or real?

Here comes the science!

The next section of the book will look at the stories, the evidence, and the artifacts and put them to the test of science. You will also find out about some of the more outrageous Bigfoot and yeti hoaxes and learn how to debunk them using scientific methods and knowledge. After you have examined the evidence, you can make up your own mind and draw your own conclusions.

THE SCIENTIFIC METHOD

Good investigators follow the scientific method when they need to establish and test a theory. The scientific method has five basic steps:

1. Make observations (comments based on studying something closely).
2. Do some background research.
3. Form a testable hypothesis. This is basically a prediction, or "educated guess," to explain the observations.
4. Conduct experiments or find evidence to support the hypothesis.
5. After thinking carefully about the evidence, draw conclusions.

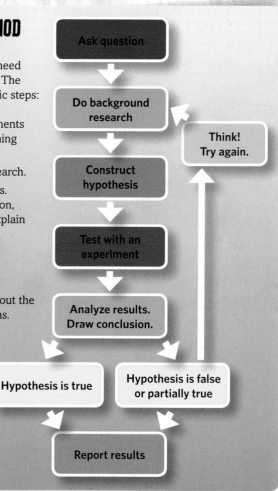

Ask question

Do background research

Construct hypothesis

Test with an experiment

Analyze results. Draw conclusion.

Think! Try again.

Hypothesis is true

Hypothesis is false or partially true

Report results

MAN OR BEAST?

Most reports of Bigfoot and the yeti mention its great height and hairiness. As long ago as 1832, a British man named Brian H. Hodson went to Nepal. There, he saw an unknown creature that moved upright, was "covered in long, dark hair, and had no tail." But is it possible that science has yet to discover and prove the existence of a 7-foot- (2.1-meter-) tall, 600-pound (270-kilogram), strong-smelling biped?

A new species?

A cryptid is a mythological animal that has not been proven to exist yet. When a possible new species is discovered, scientists use a method to decide what family it belongs to.

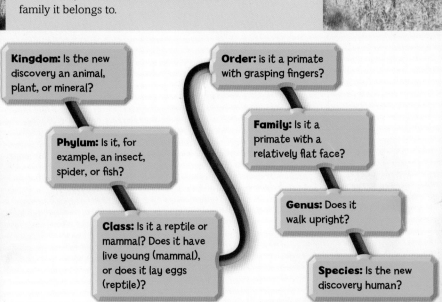

Kingdom: Is the new discovery an animal, plant, or mineral?

Order: is it a primate with grasping fingers?

Phylum: Is it, for example, an insect, spider, or fish?

Family: Is it a primate with a relatively flat face?

Class: Is it a reptile or mammal? Does it have live young (mammal), or does it lay eggs (reptile)?

Genus: Does it walk upright?

Species: Is the new discovery human?

So, what sort of creature are the Bigfoot and yeti? Scientists called anthropologists study human development.

Part of the human family?

In 1980, Chinese scientists discovered the pickled hands and feet of Xu Fudi's yeti (see the story on page 10). These were found to be from known animals. However, the scientists also found dens covered with leaves and branches. These were not like normal animal shelters and could have been used by human-like creatures.

THE MISSING LINK?

In 1859, Charles Darwin published a theory that challenged what people thought about creation. He believed that humans were evolved from apes and not created in the way suggested in the Bible, but he could not prove the last stage of development. Today, some people believe that Bigfoot and the yeti could be the stage or "missing link" between apes and humans in Darwin's theory of evolution—a kind of prehistoric man.

▼ Charles Darwin believed that humans evolved from apes over millions of years.

Bigfoot-busters!

All over the world, people are looking for giant ape-like creatures. Governments and rich individuals have funded Bigfoot and yeti expeditions in a bid to be the first to prove their existence.

A life's work

Austrian climber Reinhold Messner spent years exploring the Himalayas after claiming to have encountered a yeti in Tibet in 1986. He explored and trekked across inhospitable landscapes, talked to locals, and investigated so-called yeti relics in monasteries. But he did not find conclusive proof of the yeti's existence.

Remote landscapes

One of the biggest problems facing yeti and Bigfoot investigators is the size of the areas they are searching in. The Himalayas cover an area of over 230,000 square miles (595,000 square kilometers), while Bigfoots have been reported all over North America. To date, there are vast areas still to be explored.

Unreliable witnesses

Most people who claim to have seen a Bigfoot or yeti have nearly always been on their own. Scientific proof needs evidence to say whether something is true, not just stories. Because the descriptions in the reports vary, investigators are not exactly sure what they are looking for.

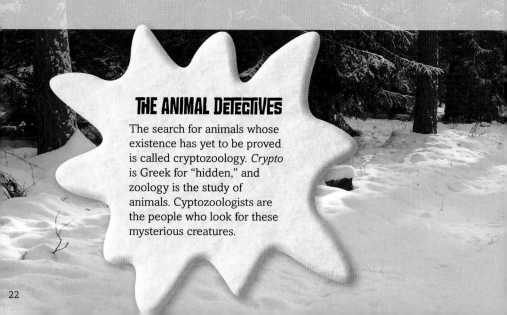

THE ANIMAL DETECTIVES

The search for animals whose existence has yet to be proved is called cryptozoology. *Crypto* is Greek for "hidden," and zoology is the study of animals. Cyptozoologists are the people who look for these mysterious creatures.

▲ In the 1950s, the French *Radar* magazine published a story about a "man of the snow" seen in the Tibetan Himalayas.

IS SEEING BELIEVING?

In Oregon, Bigfoot-hunters have set up infrared cameras on trees, hoping to get photographic evidence of the creature. But are photographs always reliable as evidence?

Faking photos

Today, it is easy to fake what is seen in photographs using computers and image manipulation software. Even in the 1950s and 1960s, it was possible to make fake but convincing pictures. Using different colored lenses and filming from a distance made the images less clear. Some were so well done that scientists still debate them.

Heat cameras

An infrared camera creates images by measuring the temperature of objects. So far, no infrared photos of Bigfoots or yeti have been taken, but it could only be a matter of time…

▼ Cameras in the wild can capture amazing close-up images.

"I'll take pictures and shake hands if I meet him."

– *Japanese yeti expedition leader Yoshiteru Takahashi*

Making sense of nonsense?

Which way is the water flowing in the picture to the right? Look carefully. Can you tell which way is up and which way is down?

The theory that we see what we want to is called involuntary vision manipulation. Our brains try to make sense of what we are looking at, so if we want to see a Bigfoot or a yeti, we will, even when it is probably a bear. The artist M. C. Escher explored the way our brains work in his pictures. Could it be that "Bigfoot-spotters" are simply seeing what they want to see?

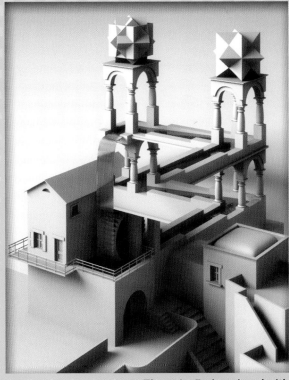

▲ The artist Escher played with perspective to challenge how we look at things.

▼ This 1995 photograph taken in Nepal in the Himalayas is considered a fake. What do you think?

BIG FOOTPRINTS, BIG NEWS?

As you have read, many Bigfoot and yeti reports are based on people seeing giant footprints. Some prints are too vague to be conclusive, but a few are so detailed that they baffle the experts. So far, none of these has been identified as belonging to any known species, but the investigations go on.

The Everest yeti?

In 1951, Eric Shipton and a team of climbers were attempting to scale Mount Everest when they came across gigantic footprints in the ice. They did not make it to the top of the mountain, but that didn't matter, because they got the photographic find of the century!

Sixty-year-old debate

Scientists still debate and ask questions of Shipton's "yeti" evidence today. Is the heel too narrow to be a bear? Are the toes too spaced apart to be a human? Are there two big toes? Look closely at the photograph—what do you think? Could the prints be real? How could they have been faked without leaving human tracks alongside them?

More proof?

In December 2007, at Mount Everest, a U.S. television team is filming. They see enormous footprints like the ones Eric Shipton saw. The team make casts of the prints, and these are later examined back in the United States by Dr. Jeffrey Meldrum, an expert in anatomy and anthropology. After detailed study, he concludes they could be evidence of a new species.

Wind effect

Many scientists believe that the prints are caused by wind erosion and runoff produced by melting snow. Wind picks up surface snow particles and distributes them over a wide area. In this way, a bear print would become larger than it originally was.

▲ Could this footprint be proof of the yeti?

Mistaken identity?

Misidentification of Himalayan wildlife has been suggested as an explanation for some Yeti sightings. The Chu-Teh monkey, the Tibetan blue bear, and the Himalayan brown bear are all possible "yetis." Some people even think the yeti could be an orangutan!

Changing continents?

Orangutans are great apes that live on the islands of Borneo and Sumatra in the South China Sea. Some zoologists think that a number of orangutans may have stayed on mainland Asia before the continents separated and drifted apart millions of years ago. What do you think? And how does the yeti find enough food to survive in the snowy Himalayas?

▲ The Himalayan or Asiatic black bear is one of the animals that might be identified as the yeti.

The giant ape theory

Some scientists, such as Grover Krantz and Geoffrey Bourne, thought that Bigfoot could be a present-day relative of an extinct giant ape called *Gigantopithecus*. This huge creature roamed across what is now China, India, and Vietnam. *Gigantopithecus* fossils found in China show that it was tall and strong and walked on two feet.

Scientists know that many species of animals migrated across the Bering land bridge between Asia and North America before the continents drifted apart. Krantz and Bourne think that *Gigantopithecus* did, too, which is their explanation for why giant ape-men are seen across Asia and North America.

The climber's conclusion

After years of investigating, Reinhold Messner concluded that the yeti was the endangered Himalayan brown bear. This bear can walk upright as well as on all fours. He reported, "All evidence points to a nocturnal species of brown bear… This bear can run, climb, and track far better than a man."

PLEASE
DO NOT
CLIMB IN THE
EXHIBIT

▲ This is a re-creation of what *Gigantopithecus* looked like. It is in the Museum of Man in San Diego, California.

UNDER THE MICROSCOPE

Yeti fingers and scalps and Bigfoot body parts and pelts have all been presented as evidence of the creatures' existence, but do they stand up to scientific study?

In 1960, mountaineer Edmund Hillary went to Nepal with zoologist Marlin Perkins to look for the yeti. At Khumjung monastery, they were given an alleged yeti scalp and took it back to the United States for forensic examination.

▼ This yeti scalp from Khumjung monastery was given to Edmund Hillary in 1960.

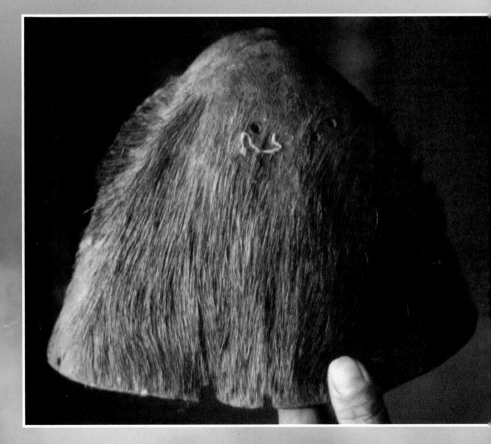

What is forensic science?

Forensic science uses a range of different laboratory tests on things like bones, hair, and skin to build up a profile of what something looks like.

Every living thing has its own special code, called its DNA. This tells us what family and group it belongs to in addition to giving us individual details such as eye or hair color.

Perfect match?

In 2008, scientists in Oxford, England, analyzed the DNA of "yeti hairs" that had been collected in Northeast India. They found similarities between these hairs and the ones on Edmund Hillary's "yeti scalp." They then matched the hair DNA to that of a Himalayan goat called the Goral, which proved the specimens were fake. So far, however, DNA tests on some Bigfoot hair samples do not match any known animal. Using the scientific method, what could this mean?

▲ There are many bones that people claim are yeti relics. What do you think?

Myth-buster

The bare bones

In 2011, scientists at Edinburgh Zoo in Scotland solved the 50-year-old mystery of a yeti finger that was smuggled out of Nepal by movie actor James Stewart. Dr. Rob Ogden, an expert in genetics, analyzed a DNA sample taken from the finger and found it to be a human bone.

Sound waves and thin air

Lots of people report hearing a strange sound when they encounter a Bigfoot or yeti. In fact, sounds are more often reported than sightings. What could be the explanation behind this? Can the sounds be explained?

Making waves

When a sound wave meets an obstacle, some of the sound is reflected back from the surface of the obstacle and some of the sound passes into it. Here, it is absorbed or transmitted through the material. So, the assumed howl or cry of a Bigfoot or yeti might be distorted as sound waves travel through trees, echo across valleys, or are absorbed into the landscape. In other words, don't believe everything you hear—if you think you hear a Bigfoot, it might just be the distorted sounds of a bear, wolf, or even a dog.

Importance of oxygen

Most sightings of the yeti occur high up in the mountains. At 9,850 feet (3,000 meters) and over, there is less oxygen in the air. This makes the air "thin," which means that you are high up, or "at altitude." Low levels of oxygen can affect people's brain function, vision, judgment, and perceptions of what is around them. The retina of the eye requires large amounts of oxygen, so at altitude, day and night vision often becomes blurred. So, do you think climbers' tales of the yeti are likely to be reliable?

◄ Many high-altitude climbers use oxygen to keep them thinking and seeing clearly.

SCIENCE VERSUS CULTURE

Imagine being the first person to find conclusive, undisputed, scientific proof of the existence of Bigfoot. You would be world famous, just as Roger Patterson and Robert Gimlin have been since their Bigfoot film of 1967.

It is October 20, 1967, a clear, brisk day in Bluff Creek, California. Two amateur Bigfoot-hunters are filming, hoping to catch a sighting. All of a sudden, out of the trees walks a Bigfoot!

▼ The 1967 Patterson and Gimlin film is still being analyzed and debated today.

Fake film?

Many people think the film is a hoax, but no one has ever proved this. Biomechanics expert Dmitri Donskoy studies how bodies move. He believes that the creature's walk is different from how a man in an ape suit moves, which might suggest the footage is real. However, other scientists, such as anthropologists David J. Daegling and Daniel O. Schmitt, say it is impossible to be 100 percent sure either way, and more evidence is needed.

Myth-buster

Dressing up the facts

In 2002, a costume shop owner claimed he had sent an ape suit to Roger Patterson in 1967. Another man, Bob Heironimus, further claimed he had worn the ape suit for the film. Do these "confessions" make good evidence? Do they prove the film is a fake? Think about the science and the proof required.

MONSTER MANIA!

Everybody loves a giant! Huge ape-men and hairy monsters can be box-office gold. *Star Wars*, *Monsters Inc.*, and *Bigfoot* are just some of the movies to have characters inspired by Bigfoot and the yeti.

MIND OVER MATTER?

Cultures across the Himalayas and East Asia have yeti figures and have long believed in their powers. Pelts, bones, and fur supposedly from yetis are highly prized by Tibetan people as charms to ward off evil spirits. So, how does science approach stories concerned with belief?

▲ These monks are dancing to honor the yeti at the Mani Rimdu festival.

A question of belief

Stories of Bigfoot and yeti encounters can seep into local legend, and so people believe them. Some anthropologists attribute yeti belief to superstition in a bogeyman figure.

In the Himalayan country of Bhutan, it is believed that yetis can become invisible and that they have the power to make snow melt. Some people also say that yetis have backward-facing feet so that they can confuse people who try to follow them. Is that why no one can find them? And does believing in something make it real? What does a scientific approach say? Psychologists suggest that humans believe in scary creatures as a way to protect themselves and survive against the unknown.

> "The myth of the yeti will survive for as long as the natives imagine it as more than just an animal. The tales fulfill longings and dreams... and fears, and provide the awe of something with superior power."
>
> *– Climber and explorer Reinhold Messner*

Based on the evidence so far, do you agree with this quotation?

▶ **In some parts of the United States, drivers are warned to look out for Bigfoot (also known as Sasquatch) crossings!**

SCIENCE FACT OR SCIENCE FICTION?

The existence—or nonexistence—of a giant ape-man inspires strong reactions. Many scientists believe it is impossible for such a creature to exist in such harsh environments or to have remained undiscovered for so long. Others think the evidence strongly suggests they could exist.

Believers and skeptics

Primate expert Jane Goodall has said she would not be surprised if an undiscovered primate like Bigfoot exists. Dr. Jeff Meldrum believes Bigfoot almost certainly exists, but that we just have not fully proven it yet. However, disbelievers, or skeptics, think that all the footprints and reported sightings can be explained scientifically. But what do you think so far?

> "People from very different backgrounds and different parts of the world have described very similar creatures behaving in similar ways and uttering some strikingly similar sounds...As far as I am concerned, the existence of hominids of this sort is a very real probability."
>
> – Jane Goodall, author of In the Shadow of Man, one of the most respected books about chimpanzees and apes

Mud print

Gifford Pinchot National Forest, in Washington state, is a huge national park that covers over 2,000 square miles (5,300 square kilometers). In September 2000, a group of researchers discovered part of a body print in the mud in Skookum Meadow. They made a plaster cast of it.

A number of scientists studied the cast. Some believe it shows the leg, hip, thigh, heel, and ankle of a Bigfoot. However, others think it is simply the print of an elk lying on its side. The analysis continues.

▼ Jeff Meldrum is a leading expert about Sasquatch, or Bigfoot.

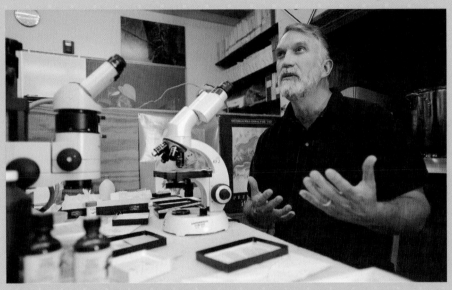

Recent Bigfoot sightings by state

U.S. state	Number of Bigfoot sightings
Oregon	808
Washington	151
California	94
Idaho	25
Florida	20
Ohio	13
Michigan	13
Texas	9
Oklahoma	7
Montana	6

Famous hoaxes

Dressing up in a gorilla suit must be fun, as many Bigfoot pranksters spend lots of time and effort in making photographs, footprints, and films realistic. Read on to find out about some of the more outrageous hoaxes.

Bluffing at Bluff Creek

In 1958, Jerry Crew was working on a construction site in Bluff Creek, California. Sets of large footprints appeared overnight. After not being taken seriously about what he was seeing, Jerry brought in his friend, Bob Titmus, to cast the prints in plaster. Scientists and the public debated about what they could be, but most dismissed them as fake.

Over 40 years later, in 2002, a man named Ray Wallace died. His family came forward and identified him as the "Bigfoot of Bluff Creek" prankster. They had the 16-inch- (41-centimeter-) long wooden feet he used to make the prints. The feet matched the cast exactly.

▶ How easy do you think it would be to fake footprints like this?

Frozen fake

On July 9, 2008, Rick Dyer and Matthew Whitton posted a video online claiming that they had discovered the body of a dead Bigfoot in a forest in northern Georgia. Major news networks around the world covered the story, and reporters were sent to a press conference.

The alleged Bigfoot body was presented in a block of ice in a freezer. When the contents were thawed, it was discovered that the hair was not real, the head was hollow, and the feet were rubber. Dyer and Whitton later admitted it was a theatrical hoax.

▼ The famous "frozen yeti" hoax fooled many until the yeti was thawed.

CAN THE MYSTERY BE SOLVED?

After hundreds of reported sightings, dozens of unexplained footprints, fuzzy photographs, stinky smells, and horrible howls, are we any closer to solving the mystery of Bigfoot?

> "Given the scientific evidence that I have examined, I'm convinced there's a creature out there that is yet to be identified."
>
> – Dr. Jeff Meldrum, professor of anatomy and anthropology, Idaho State University

New species

Science has already proven the existence of creatures thought to be extinct—for example, the white rhino in the early 1900s and the wood bison in the 1960s. Lots of scientists think that a giant human-ape could exist, and there is no shortage of people looking to finally prove or disprove the theory.

Yeti university

Currently, Russian and American scientists are working together to find the yeti in remote parts of Russia. And a Russian yeti institute is even being planned! The search continues...

In 2012, scientists at the University of Oxford, in England, began a yeti and Bigfoot project. The team asked anyone with evidence of either creature to send in their "proof." The scientists will perform DNA analyses on the samples. Geneticist Bryan Sykes said, "I'm challenging and inviting the cryptozoologists to come up with the evidence."

> ## "Whoever does find it will have the discovery of the century."
>
> *– Russell Mittermeier, president of Conservation International*

So, what do you think? Are you a believer or a skeptic? What is your evidence? If Bigfoots and yeti are discovered, what will happen to them? Should we leave them alone? And, perhaps most importantly, do you really want to know for sure?

◀ The search for this mysterious creature continues...

TIMELINE

326 BCE
Alexander the Great sets out with his Greek army to conquer the Indus Valley. He is told the yeti cannot breathe at low altitudes, so he never sees one.

1811
David Thompson finds footprints 14 inches (35 centimeters) long and 8 inches (20 centimeters) wide in the snow near Jasper, Alberta, Canada

1832
First recorded sighting of the yeti by Nepalese villagers

1910
Two miners are found with their heads chopped off in Nahanni Valley, Canada. The deaths are blamed on a Bigfoot.

1924
Miners are attacked in their cabin in Washington state

1951
Eric Shipton takes photographs of large footprints in the snow at 19,685 feet (6,000 meters) above sea level

1950s
The Pangboche hand and scalp are examined and found to be fake

1957
Albert Ostman claims a family of Bigfoots kidnapped him in 1924

1957
The government of Nepal passes a law that forbids all foreign mountaineers from killing, injuring, or capturing a yeti

1958
Jerry Crew finds large footprints at Bluff Creek, California

1960
Edmund Hillary and Marlin Perkins bring a supposed yeti scalp to the United States for examination

1961
The government of Nepal make the yeti its national symbol

1967
Bigfoot is "filmed" in Bluff Creek, California, by Roger Patterson and Bob Grimlin

1992
Julian Freeman-Atwood finds yeti footprints on a Mongolian glacier that no one has climbed for 30 years.

1998
Reinhold Messner, the world-famous climber, concludes over 30 years of hunting for the Yeti

2004
Four young people see a 7-foot- (2.1-meter-) tall creature with white hair and red eyes in a wooded area near the town of Chalfont, Pennsylvania

2005
The Sakteng Wildlife Sanctuary is created in Bhutan to protect yeti habitat

2007
American archaeologist Josh Gates uses infrared cameras near Mount Everest. He and his team find a series of large footprints high up in the mountains and report hearing a strange noise.

2011
An international conference on yetis is held in Russia

SUMMING UP
THE SCIENCE

There are two main theories that attempt to explain the possible existence of Bigfoot and the yeti. One follows Charles Darwin's idea of a human-ape (see pages 20 and 21), while the other explains the mysterious noises (see pages 32 and 33). The theories divide scientists. Which side are you on?

Darwin and the giant ape theory

Charles Darwin's studies showed how similar humans and apes are, and how 4-foot- (1.2-meter-) tall creatures developed into bipeds. The extinct *Gigantopithecus* proves that, at one point, there were giant human-like apes walking around on two feet. Putting these two theories together, some people think that Bigfoot and the yeti could be a kind of prehistoric man—the missing link between apes and humans.

Sound waves

All noises create sound waves. If an animal in a forest makes a sound, the sound waves have to pass through and around many obstacles, such as trees. The sound waves get longer and shorter as they reflect and bounce off the surface of the trees, and the sound is changed. So, what might sound strange and weird is actually just a distortion of a common or known sound.

GLOSSARY

altitude high place or region

anatomy structure of the body

anthropologist person who studies human development

anthropology study of human development

artifact object made by a human

Bering land bridge thin strip of land that joined North America and Asia millions of years ago

biomechanics study of body movements

biped creature that walks on two feet

cast molded object

cautionary tale story giving a warning about something

continent one of Earth's seven landmasses

cryptid creature or plant whose existence has been suspected but not proved

cryptozoology study of legendary creatures

debunk show something to be false

distorted altered, changed, or different than normal

DNA substance carrying a living thing's genetic information

erosion weather wearing away at a surface

evolve develop over time

forensic applying science to solving mysteries or crimes

geneticist expert in the physical characteristics of humans

genetics study of inherited physical characteristics

hominid member of the primate family, like a human

hypothesis explanation for an occurrence or problem that needs evidence or testing before it can be accepted as true

infrared light or radiation wave that cannot be seen by humans

inhospitable difficult to live or work in

migrate move from place to place

monastery community of monks

pelt skin of an animal with the hair, fur, or wool still attached

perception using senses to gain information about the surroundings

primate animals like monkeys, apes, and humans

prospecting looking for gold

relic old object from the past

sane healthy; not crazy

Sherpa Himalayan group of people

skeptic nonbeliever, doubter

supernatural not of the natural world

superstition belief in something that has no basis in science

undisputed unquestionable, definite

unnerved nervous, scared

zoologist scientist who studies animals

FIND OUT MORE

BOOKS

Teitelbaum, Michael. *Bigfoot Caught on Film: And Other Monster Sightings!* (Mystery Files). New York: Franklin Watts, 2008.

Theisen, Paul. *Bigfoot* (Unexplained). Minneapolis: Bellwether Media, 2011.

Townsend, John. *Strange Creatures* (Amazing Mysteries). Mankato, Minn.: Smart Apple Media, 2010.

WEB SITES

animal.discovery.com/tv-shows/finding-bigfoot
Find out lots of information and watch interesting videos about Bigfoot on this Animal Planet web site.

www.bermuda-triangle.org/html/yeti.html
This site has information about all sorts of unexplained mysteries, including Bigfoot and the yeti.

campfire.andycamper.com/the-weird-outdoors-is-Bigfoot-real
See the evidence and find out why some people are convinced Bigfoot is out there. You can also learn how to track an animal on this fun kids' site.

MOVIES

Harry and the Hendersons (Amblin Entertainment,1987).
This timeless family classic "proves" that Bigfoot is not just a legend.

Monsters Inc. (Pixar, 2001).
This fun animated movie has a yeti in a starring role!

PLACES TO VISIT

If you ever get the chance to visit Oregon or Washington state, visit the forest parks: this is classic Bigfoot country. But remember, think like a scientist!

In the town of Felton, California, there is the Bigfoot Museum. See if you can sift through the evidence and decide what is real and what is likely to be a hoax.

If you are lucky enough to go to Nepal, you could stay in the Yak and Yeti Hotel in Kathmandu!

In the city of Pokhara in Nepal, there is the exciting Mountain Museum, which has displays about the yeti, including some amazing photographs. View the evidence and decide what it suggests.

TOPICS TO RESEARCH

Choose something you liked in this book and take your Bigfoot and yeti scientific investigations further!

- You could visit your local library to find out about different "wild men" that are said to exist in other parts of the world.

- See how hard it is to fake footprints in the ground, leaving no trace that you were ever there.

INDEX